BUILD A DOODLE CITY

STEP-BY-STEP LINE DRAWINGS TO IMPROVE VISUAL PERCEPTION

Written and Illustrated by Beverly Armstrong

The Learning Works

Copyright © 1985
The Learning Works, Inc.
Santa Barbara, California 93160

All rights reserved.
No form of this work may be reproduced or transmitted or recorded without written permission from the publisher.

Printed in the United States of America.

Introduction

Build a Doodle City presents step-by-step visual patterns for creating simple line drawings of people and objects found in and around a city. The purpose of this book is not to teach children how to draw but to improve their visual perception, develop their fine motor skills, and give them hours of pleasurable practice in perceiving proportions and recognizing relationships.

The drawings in **Build a Doodle City** are arranged in order of difficulty. Below each drawing is an idea for "more doodle fun." These ideas encourage doodlers to add something to their drawings and/or to use what they have drawn in some creative way.

Build a Doodle City is easy for kids to use at home, in the classroom, or while traveling. No special instructions are needed. Just provide colored pencils, crayons, or felt-tipped pens. And because doodlers draw on separate sheets of paper, **Build a Doodle City** can be enjoyed over and over again.

fire hydrant

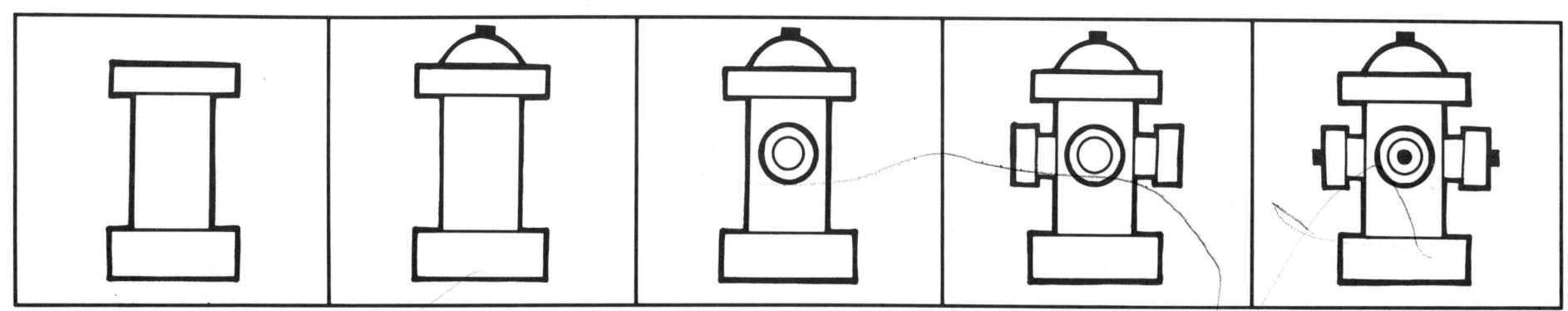

More doodle fun:
Color your fire hydrant red or yellow.

traffic signal

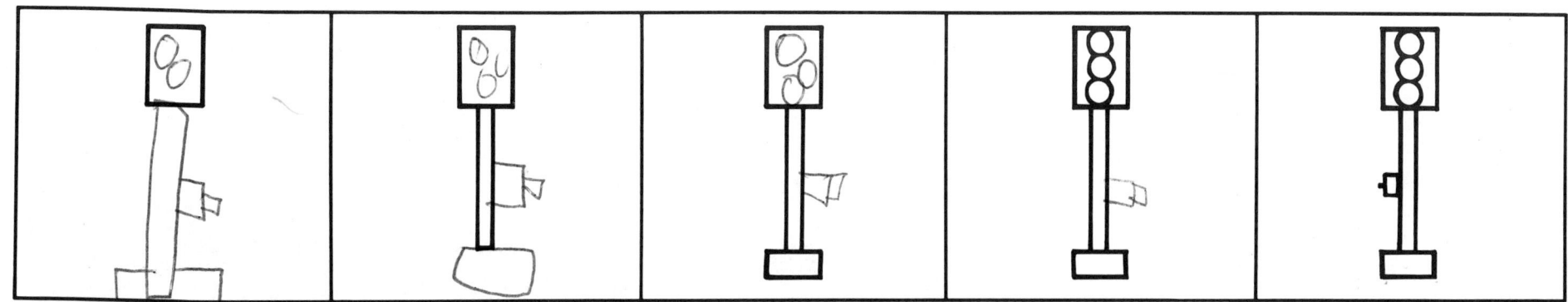

More doodle fun:
Color the lights on your traffic signal red, yellow, and green.

mailbox

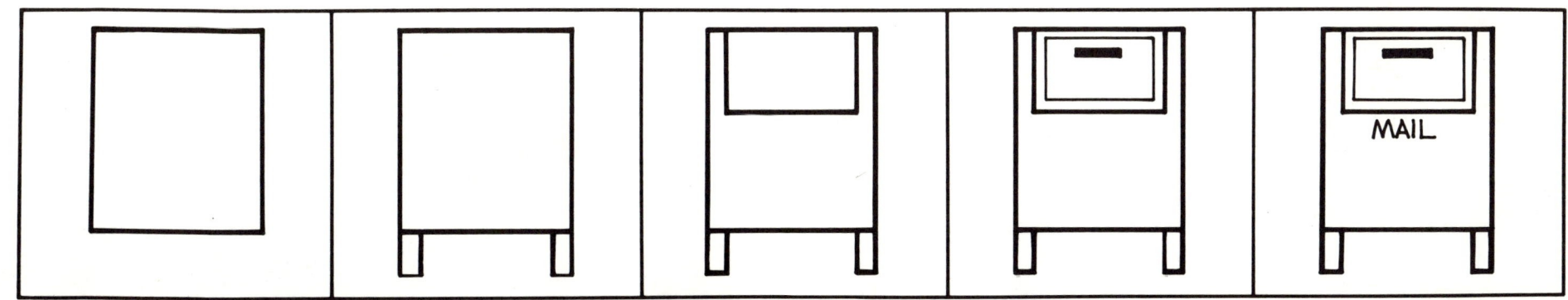

More doodle fun:
Draw a cat peeking out from behind the mailbox.

blimp

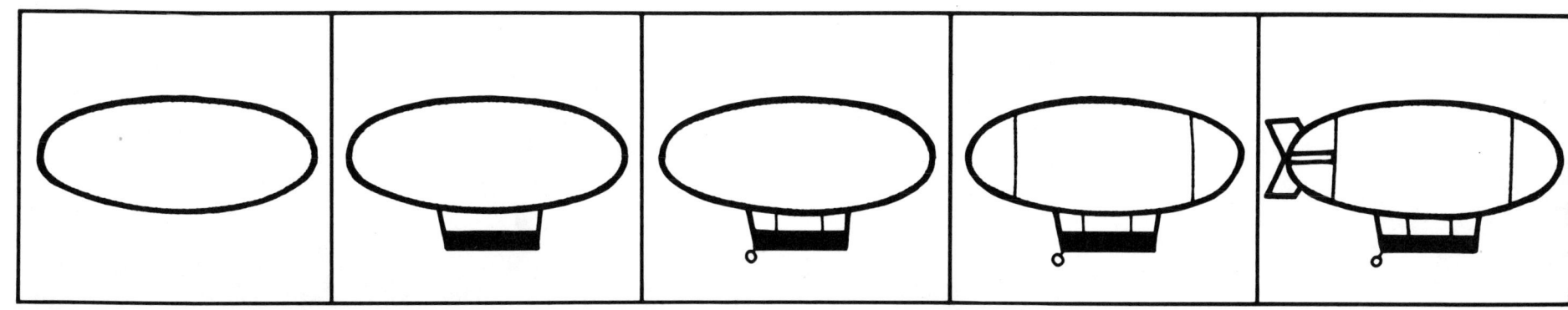

More doodle fun:
Write a message on the side of your blimp.

parking meter

More doodle fun:
Draw yourself putting money in the meter.

railroad sign

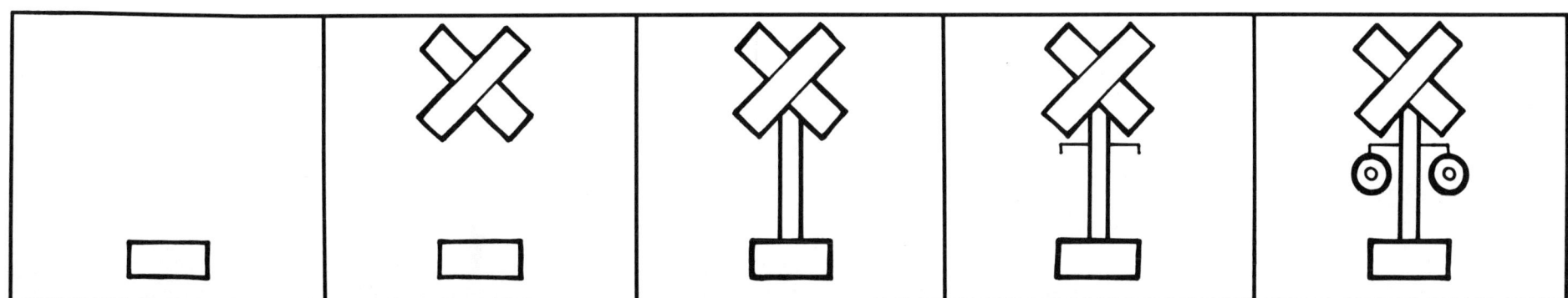

More doodle fun:
Draw train tracks behind your railroad sign.

gasoline pump

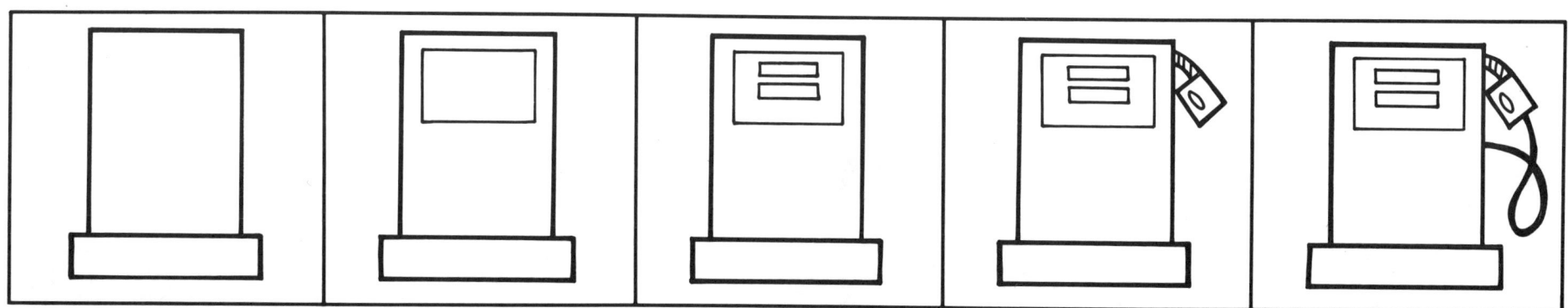

More doodle fun:

Write the name of a brand of gasoline on your pump.

crane

More doodle fun:
Give your crane a heavy load to lift.

helicopter

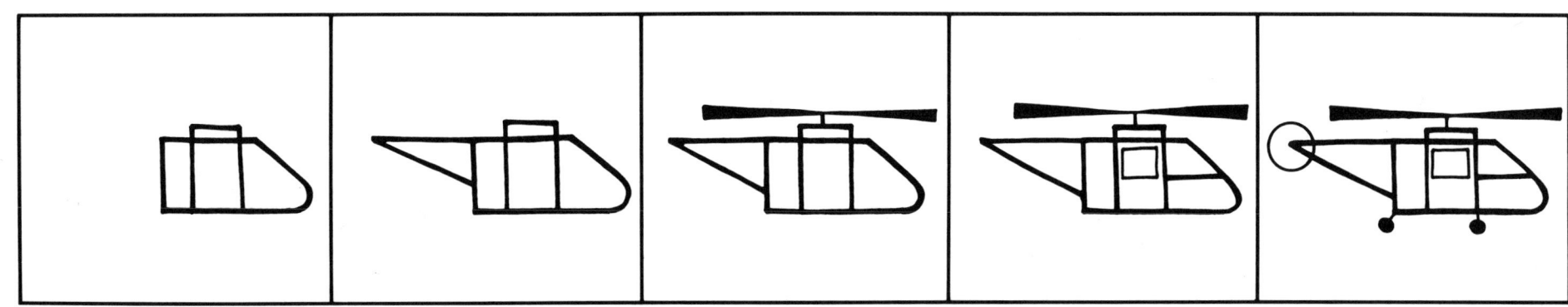

More doodle fun:
Draw a helicopter landing on a building.

telephone

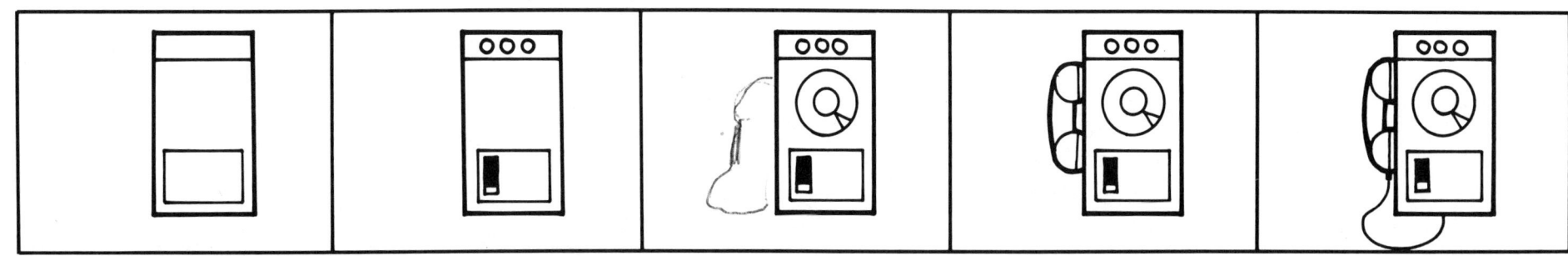

More doodle fun:
Make a life-size picture of a telephone. Cut it out and hang it in your room.

truck

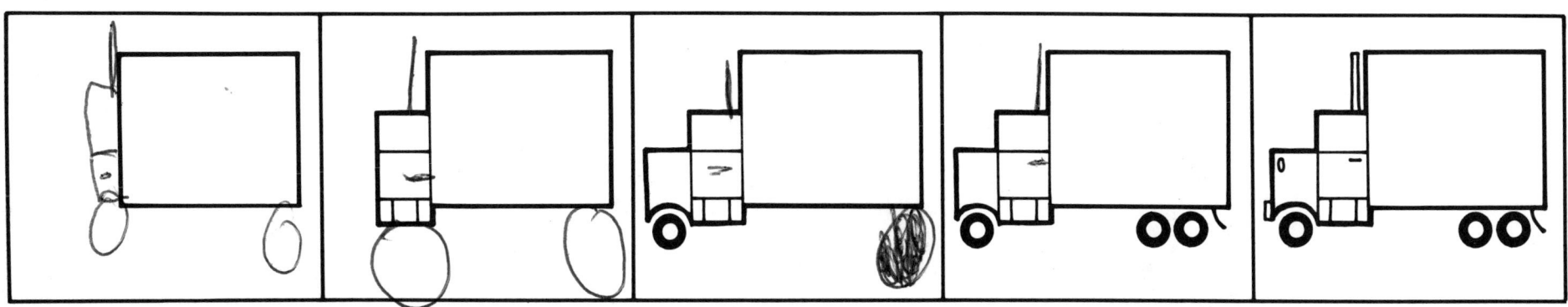

More doodle fun:

Draw a picture on the truck to show what it is carrying.

street sweeper

More doodle fun:
Draw some trash in front of the street sweeper.

ambulance

More doodle fun:
Draw a driver in your ambulance.

taxi

More doodle fun:
Draw a police car following your taxi.

fire engine

More doodle fun:

Draw a person being lifted high by the fire engine.

bus

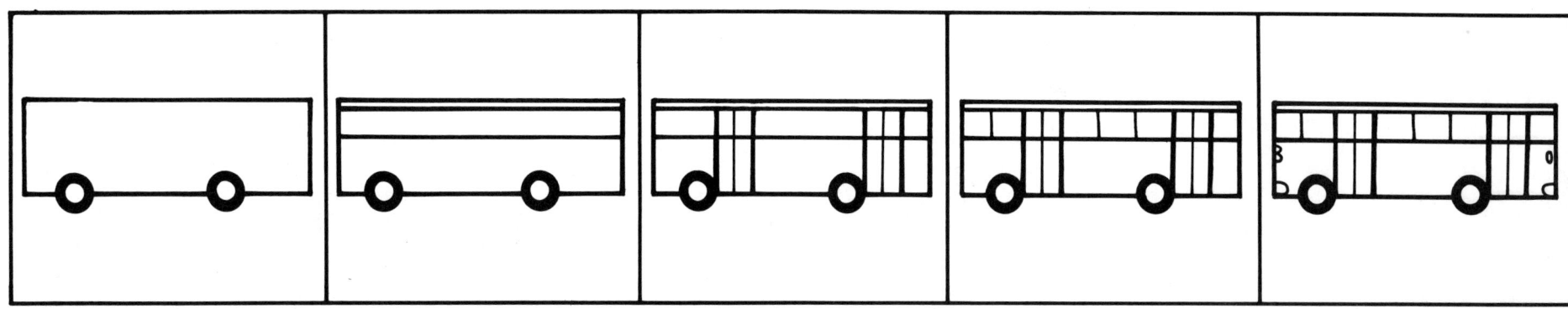

More doodle fun:
Draw faces in the windows of your bus.

power lines

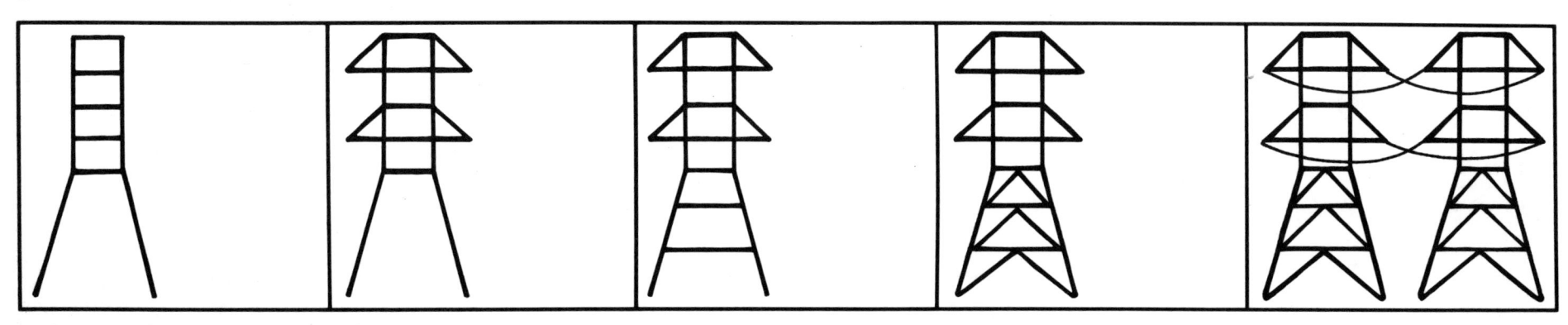

More doodle fun:

Draw a sign near your power lines telling people to stay away.

apartment building

More doodle fun:

Draw someone flying a kite on the roof of your building.

movie theater

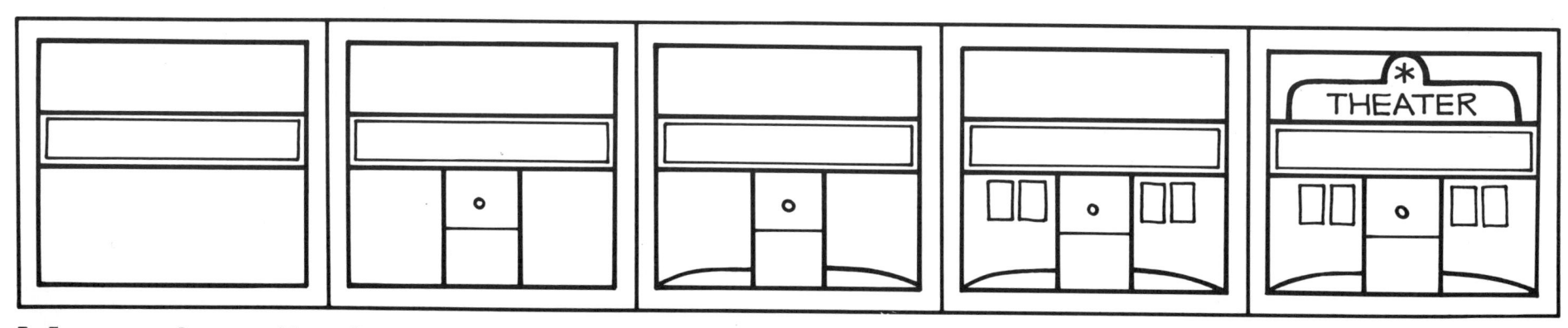

More doodle fun:

Write the name of a movie on the front of your theater.

cafe

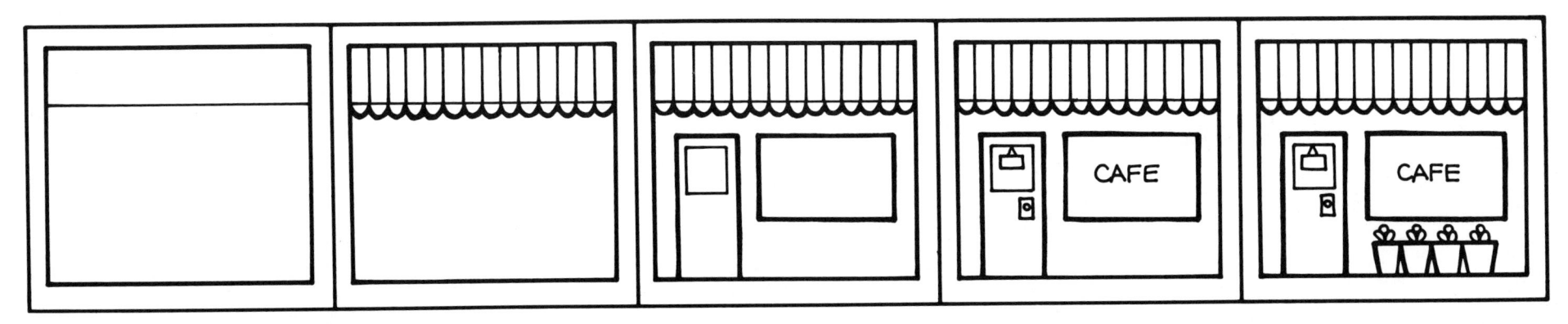

More doodle fun:

Draw a toy store, a pet store, or a candy store next to the cafe.

newsstand

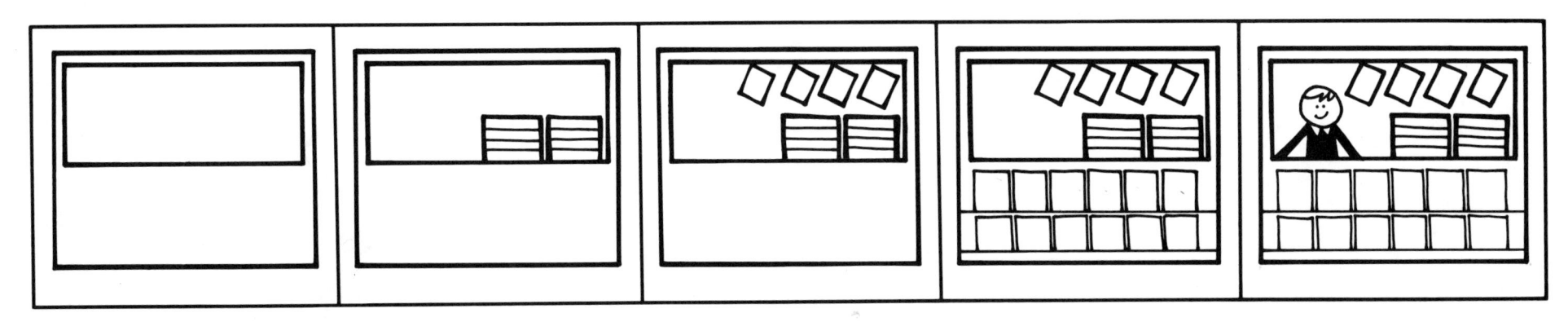

More doodle fun:

Draw a hot dog stand or a flower stand next to the newsstand.

police officer

More doodle fun:

Draw a police officer holding a sign that says STOP.

fire fighter

More doodle fun:

Connect your fire fighter's hose to a fire hydrant. Look on page 3.

mail carrier

More doodle fun:
Draw a mail carrier putting a letter in your mailbox.

street repairman

More doodle fun:

Draw a repairman making a hole in the street.

ice cream vendor

More doodle fun:

Add an umbrella to your vendor's cart.

trees

More doodle fun:

Draw a park with several kinds of trees.

fences and walls

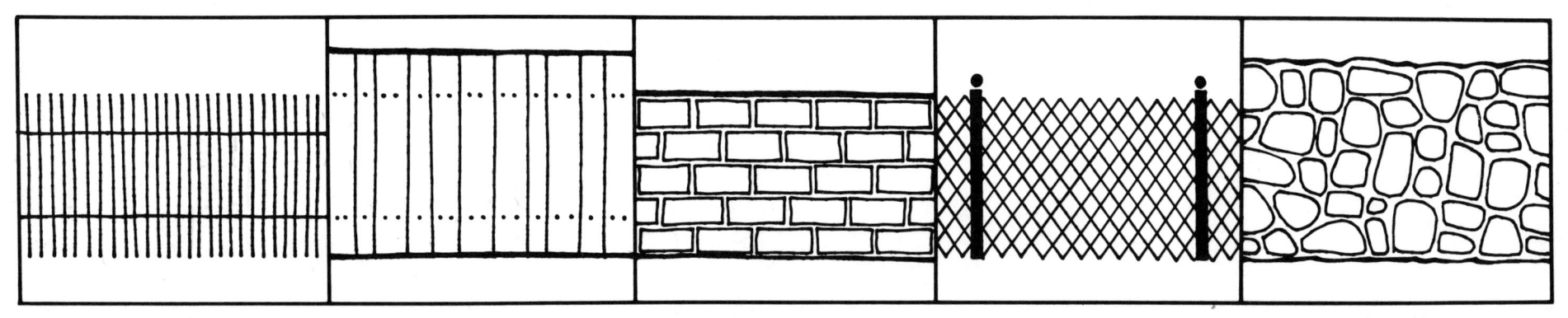

More doodle fun:

Draw a person or an animal looking over a wall or through a fence.

playground equipment

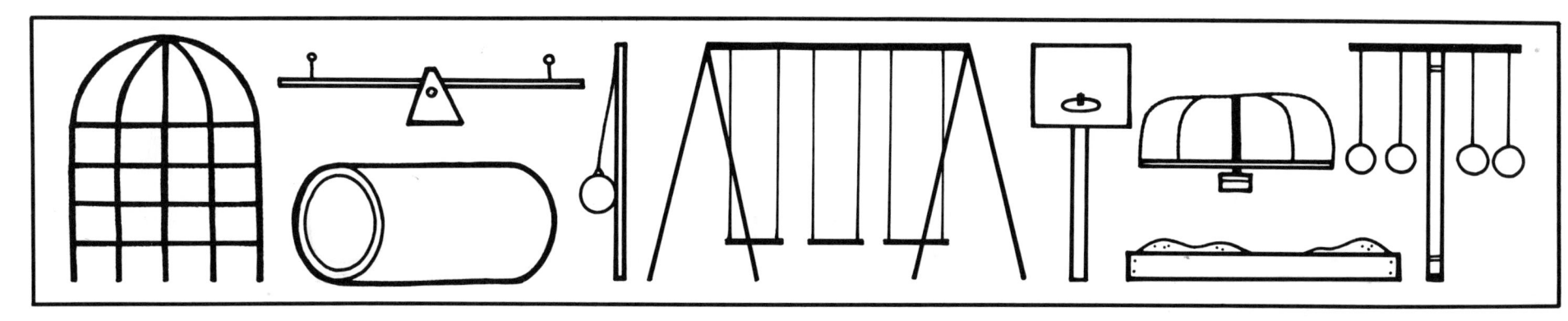

More doodle fun:

Design a playground with all of your favorite pieces of equipment.

more city things

More doodle fun:

Make a big mural of a city.